The Original Icon of Our Lady of Perpetual Help
Venerated in the Church of Saint Alphonsus, Rome

OUR LADY
OF PERPETUAL HELP

THE ICON, FAVORS AND SHRINES

Edited by Noel Londoño, C.Ss.R.

Translated by Damián Wall, C.Ss.R.

Liguori
ONE LIGUORI DRIVE
LIGUORI MO 63057-9999

Imprimi Potest:
Richard Thibodeau, C.Ss.R.
Provincial, Denver Province
The Redemptorists

ISBN 0-7648-0938-5
© 2002, Liguori Publications
Printed in Spain
02 03 04 05 06   5 4 3 2 1

This work has been prepared by a team of Redemptorist Missionaries and published on the occasion of the third centenary of the birth of Saint Alphonsus Liguori, a great singer of the Glories of Mary.

Grateful acknowledgment is made to William Creede, C.Ss.R., *Make Her Known,* published in Australia; several parts of the pamphlet are used in the first part of this book. Argemiro Gallego for the text of the *Short Novena.*

Previously published in June 1998 in Rome. The collaboration of the following Redemptorist Missionaries has made this book possible: Francisco Ceballos, Luis Aníbal Arias, Noel Londoño.

Photographs: CssR Roma: covers, 25, 32-33; CssR Porto: p. 9; CssR Bogotá: p. 12; CssR Chile: p. 28; CssR Manila: p. 29; CssR Singapore: p. 36; J.R.: p. 40; N.L.: p. 57.

To order, call 1-800-325-9521
www.liguori.org
www.catholicbooksonline.com

PREFACE

Those that love Mary call her Mother. It could be said that there is no other name to call her, since she brought us to life on Calvary, when she offered her Son for our redemption.
(ST. ALPHONSUS: The Glories of Mary)

Among Christians, the title "Perpetual Help" is one of the better known titles of the Mother of God, especially among the most needy and afflicted who feel the need of being loved and protected. The original picture is an Eastern icon that represents the Virgin of the Passion. This icon was painted to inspire our hope and prayers. Its spiritual message far surpasses its artistic beauty.

An icon is much more than the representation of a person or a historical event. The icon of Perpetual Help reminds us of Mary and Jesus facing the reality of the Passion; but in a rather special way it purports to raise our consciousness of the mysteries of Redemption in Christ and of the intercession of Mary in favor of the followers of Jesus. Perpetual Help is a representation of Mary, but more - it is a reflection on Christ, the Redeemer in the arms of Mary.

Only with an attitude of faith and prayer can one admire this icon. The expression on Mary's face is that of a mother that knows pain and yet, offers her help unconditionally.

With serenity and tenderness, she invites us to accept the Will of God, even when we find in it suffering and the Cross, and to offer our lives in the service of others, as did her Son.

The following pages are an attempt to help us understand and live more intensely, the mystery of this icon and to inspire in each one of us the desire to pray with faith, in union with the multitude of Christians that daily look to the Holy Mother of God as the Virgin of the Passion and the Perpetual Help of all humanity.

Rev. JUAN MANUEL LASSO DE LA VEGA
Superior General of the Redemptorist Missionaries
Rome, March 25, 1997

I. HISTORY, TRADITION AND LEGEND

My name is Mother of Perpetual Help

No century or country can claim me.
I belong to all ages and all peoples.
Many names have been given to me. I have been called the "Virgin of the Passion", "the Golden Madonna", "the Mother of the Redemptorist Missionaries", "the Mother of Catholic homes".

The name of my own choosing is "Mother of Perpetual Help". *It is also the name by which Pope Pius IX requested the Redemptorist Missionaries to make me known.*

My story is of how Heaven hallows human happenings for purposes divine. It is a history that appears complicated and adventurous, but seen "from above" it is a simple, straight line drawn through human history.

It is the story of an unknown artist, a repentant thief, a curious little girl, an abandoned church, an old religious and a Pope.

And above all, it is the story of my presence in the apostolic life of the Missionaries of the Congregation of the Most Holy Redeemer.

1. *The merchant who stole "Our Lady"*

There is a tradition from the 16th century that tells us about a merchant from the isle of Crete who stole a miraculous picture from one of its churches. He hid it among his wares and set out westward. It was only through Divine Providence that he survived a wild tempest and landed on solid ground. After about a year, he arrived in Rome with his stolen picture.

It was there that he became mortally ill and looked for a friend to care for him. At his hour of death, he revealed his secret of the picture and begged his friend to return it to a church. His friend promised to fulfill this wish, but because his wife did not want to relinquish such a beautiful treasure, the friend also died without fulfilling the promise. At last, the Blessed Virgin appeared to the six year old daughter of this Roman family and told her to tell her mother and grandmother that the picture of *Holy Mary of Perpetual Help* should be placed in the Church of St. Matthew the Apostle, located between the basilicas of St. Mary Major and St. John Lateran.

The tradition relates how, after many doubts and difficulties, "the mother obeyed and after consulting with the clergy in charge of the church, the picture of the Virgin was placed in St. Matthew's, on the 27th of March, 1499". There it would be venerated during the next 300 years. Thus began the second stage of the history of the icon, and devotion to Our Mother of Perpetual Help began to spread throughout the city of Rome.

The merchant steals the icon   *and entrusts it to a family*

2. *Three Centuries in the Church of St. Matthew*

St. Matthew's Church was not grand but it possessed an enormous treasure that attracted the faithful: the icon of Our Mother of Perpetual Help. From 1739 to 1798, the church and adjacent monastery were under the care of the Irish Augustinians who had been unjustly exiled from their country and used the monastery as a formation center for their Roman Province. The young students found an asylum of peace in the presence of the Virgin of Perpetual Help while they prepared themselves for priesthood, the apostolate and martyrdom.

In 1798, war raged in Rome and the monastery and church were almost totally destroyed. Several Augustinians remained there for a few more years but eventually they, too, had to leave. Some returned to Ireland, others to new foundations in America, while the majority moved to a nearby monastery. This last group brought with them the picture of Our Lady of Perpetual Help. Thus began the third stage of her history, the "Hidden Years".

In 1819, the Irish Augustinians moved to the Church of St. Mary in Posterula, near the "Umberto I" bridge that crosses the Tiber River. With them went the "Virgin of St. Matthew's". But as "Our Lady of Grace" was already venerated in this church, the newly arrived picture was placed in a private chapel in the monastery where it remained, all but forgotten, but for Brother Augustine Orsetti, one of the original young friars from St. Matthew's.

3. *The Old Religious and the Young Altar Boy*

The years passed and it seemed that the picture that had been saved from the war that destroyed St. Matthew's Church, was about to be lost in oblivion.

A young altar boy named Michael Marchi often visited the Church of Sancta Maria in Posterula and became friends with Brother Augustine. Much later, as Father Michael, he would write:

"This good brother used to tell me with a certain air of mystery and anxiety, especially during the years 1850 and 1851, these precise words: 'Make sure you know, my son, that the image of the Virgin of St. Matthew is upstairs in the chapel: don't ever forget it... do you understand? It is a miraculous picture.' At that time the brother was almost totally blind. "What I can say about the venerable picture of the 'Virgin of St. Matthew', also called 'Perpetual Help,' is that from my childhood until I entered the Congregation (of the Redemptorists) I had always seen it above the altar of the house chapel of the Augustinian Fathers of the Irish Province at St. Mary in Posterula [...], there was no devotion to it, no decorations, not even a lamp to acknowledge its presence... it remained covered with dust and practically abandoned. Many were the times, when I served Mass there, that I would stare at it with great attention".

Brother Augustine died in 1853 at the venerable age of 86, without seeing fulfilled his desire that the Virgin of Perpetual Help be once again exposed for public veneration. His prayers and boundless confidence in the Virgin Mary seemed to have gone unanswered.

*Pope Pius IX gives the Icon of Perpetual Help
to the Redemptorist Missionaries*

4. *The Rediscovery of the Icon*

In January of 1855, the Redemptorist Missionaries purchased "Villa Caserta" in Rome, converting it into the general house for their missionary congregation that had spread to western Europe and North America. On this same property along the Via Merulana, were the ruins of the

Church and Monastery of St. Matthew. Without realizing it at the time, they had acquired the land that, many years previously, had been chosen by the Virgin as her Sanctuary between St. Mary Major and St. John Lateran.

Four months later, construction was begun on a church in honor of the Most Holy Redeemer and dedicated to Saint Alphonsus Liguori, founder of the Congregation. On December 24, 1855, a group of young men began their novitiate in the new house. One of them was Michael Marchi.

The Redemptorists were extremely interested in the history of their new property. But more so, when on February 7th, 1863, they were puzzled by the questions from a sermon given by the famous Jesuit preacher, Father Francesco Blosi, about an icon of Mary that "had been in the Church of St. Matthew on Via Merulana and was known as *The Virgin of St. Matthew,* or more correctly as *The Virgin of Perpetual Help"*.

On another occasion, the chronicler of the Redemptorist community "examining some authors who had written about Roman antiquities, found references made to the Church of St. Matthew. Among them there was a particular citation mentioning that in the church (which had been situated within the garden area of the community) there had been an ancient icon of the Mother of God that enjoyed "great veneration and fame for its miracles". Then "having told all this to the community, a dialogue began as to where they could locate the picture. Father Marchi remembered all that he had heard from old Brother Augustine Orsetti and told his confreres that he had often seen the icon and knew very well where it could be found".

5. *The Reception of the Icon by the Redemptorists*

With this new information, interest grew among the Redemptorists to know more about the icon and to retrieve it for their church. The Superior General, Father Nicholas Mauron, presented a letter to Pope Pius IX in which he petitioned the Holy See to grant them the icon of Perpetual Help and that it be placed in the newly built Church of the Most Holy Redeemer and St. Alphonsus, which was located near the site where the old Church of St. Matthew had stood. The Pope granted the request and on the back of the petition, in his own handwriting, he noted:

"December 11, 1865: The Cardinal Prefect of Propaganda will call the Superior of the community of Sancta Maria in Posterula and will tell him that it is Our desire that the image of Most Holy Mary, referred to in this petition, be again placed between Saint John and St. Mary Major; the Redemptorists shall replace it with another adequate picture".

According to tradition, this was when Pope Pius IX told the Redemptorist Superior General: *"Make Her known throughout the world!"* In January, 1866, Fathers Michael Marchi and Ernest Bresciani went to St. Mary's in Posterula to receive the picture from the Augustinians.

Then began the process of cleaning and retouching the icon. The task was entrusted to the Polish artist, Leopold Nowotny. Finally, on April 26th, 1866, the image was again presented for public veneration in the Church of St. Alphonsus on the Via Merulana.

With this event, the fourth stage of her history began: the spread of the icon throughout the world.

6. *The latest Restoration of the Icon*

In 1990, the picture of Our Mother of Perpetual Help was taken down from above the main altar to satisfy the many requests for new photographs of the icon. It was then that the serious state of deterioration of the image was discovered; the wood, as well as the paint, had suffered from environmental changes and prior attempts at restoration. The General Government of the Redemptorists decided to contract the technical services of the Vatican Museum to bring about a general restoration of the icon that would deal with the cracks and fungus that threatened irreparable damage.

The first part of the restoration consisted of a series of X-rays, infra-red images, qualitative and quantitative analyses of the paint, and other infra-red and ultra-violet tests. The results of these analyses, especially a Carbon-14 test, indicate that the wood of the icon of Perpetual Help could safely be dated from the years 1325 - 1480.

The second stage of the restoration consisted of the physical work of filling the cracks and perforations in the wood, cleaning the paint and retouching the affected sections, strengthening the structure that sustains the icon, etc. This physical intervention was limited to the absolute minimum because all restorative work, somewhat like bodily surgery, always provokes some trauma. An artistic analysis situated the pigmentation of the paint at a later date (after the 17th century); this would explain why the icon offers a synthesis of oriental and occidental elements, especially in its facial aspects.

The Virgin of Vladimir (detail)
Russian icon from the 12th century

II. THE MESSAGE OF THE ICON

As one looks at the icon of Our Mother of Perpetual Help, it is important to remember that it is *an Icon*, painted by an *anonymous artist,* in the style of *The Virgin of the Passion* that represents the *Christian mystery of Redemption.*

1. *What is an icon?*

The Greek word "*eikón*", from which comes the word "icon", means "image". Christians first used the word to describe Jesus Christ: He is the image (icon) of the invisible God (Col. 1:15; Heb. 1:3). The baptized, as well, since they are identified with Christ, are formed into the image (icon) of God and temples of the Holy Spirit (Rom. 8:14).

Nevertheless, when we speak of an icon we usually mean a representation of Christ, the Blessed Virgin or a Saint, that has been painted according to specific technical and theological norms.

An icon is much more than a simple representation of events or persons of the past. An icon makes present that which it remembers. It is a meeting point between the mystery of God and the reality of Man. An icon is not an altar decoration; an icon is an altar. This is why in the

Oriental liturgies, the icons are venerated along with the Word of God.

An icon is the fruit of prayer. The artists that painted icons would compose their pictures in an atmosphere of penance and prayer. While they worked and prayed they would think of those who one day would pray before the icon that they were painting. Icon artists were usually monks who meditated on the mysteries of God and presented in images and colors, their spiritual insights. They shared their faith and spirituality with others through art.

An icon is a object of meditation. When we come before an icon with an attitude of prayer, we can deepen our understanding of the mysterious reality that it represents and better appreciate the value of liturgical prayer. Icons were created to foster contemplation.

2. *An Unknown Artist*

The great majority of icon artists are hidden in anonymity. Among the few known that painted icons of the Virgin of the Passion, Andrea Rizo de Candia (1422-1499), of the Cretan school, is remembered as producing outstanding works of art.

The icon of Our Lady of Perpetual Help belongs to this school, but we can not indicate the exact date of its completion. What we can say with all probability, is that the artist was a monk and lived in Crete.

An ancient legend attributes the first icon of the Virgin of the Passion to St. Luke, the Evangelist. In this way the artists of Marian icons established a connection between their works and the believing community that had personally known Jesus and Mary. This legend is more a theological resource than a historical affirmation, since the techniques used in paintings of the 1st century are quite different than those used in the painting of icons. The earliest icons were painted in the 6th century, while the majority of the known icons are actually dated from the 12th century and later.

3. *The Virgin of the Passion*

The icon of Our Mother of Perpetual Help is painted on a plaque of wood that measures 54 centimeters high and 41 1/2 centimeters wide.

Throughout history it has received two basic titles. For artistic reasons and in accord with the style of image, it has been called: "The Virgin of the Passion". Icons of the Virgin of the Passion usually represent the Mother of God holding her Son Jesus and to the sides, the angels carrying the instruments of the Passion.

The other title that it bears comes from the devotion that surrounds it: "Our Mother of Perpetual Help". In our icon, the Mother of God is depicted looking tenderly at her devotees and ever ready to help them in whatever need.

The icon shows four holy figures: The Virgin Mother of God, the Christ Child and the archangels Michael and Gabriel. These personages are identified by the letters that appear in the icon.

M P - θ Y	= Mother - of God	
	(on the two sides of the upper part of the icon)	
'I C - X C	= Jesus - Christ	
	(to the right of the Christ Child's head)	
O A M	= Archangel Michael	
	(above the angel on the left, as you look at the icon)	
O A Γ	= Archangel Gabriel	
	(above the angel on the right, as you look at the icon)	

Only half of the Virgin's body is depicted but the impression is that she is standing. She wears a red tunic, a dark blue hooded cape with a green lining, a cobalt-blue head dress that covers her hair and forehead. In the center of her head on the hood, there is a star of eight golden, linear rays; next to it is a gold cross in the form of a star. The circular halo around her head, typical of the School of Crete, can be better appreciated now that the overlaid, jeweled crown that has hidden it since 1867, has been removed.

The Virgin's face is slightly inclined toward the Christ Child whom she holds in her left hand. Her larger right hand (its long fingers typical of the images that indicate the way = "Hodiguitria"), holds the hand of Jesus. With a sad tenderness, she looks not to her Son but appears to be in dialogue with whomever looks to her (universal perspective). Her almond-shaped, honey colored eyes and emphasized eye brows give her face a sense of beauty and solemnity.

The Child Jesus is depicted in full proportion. He rests in the left arm of the Virgin while His hands clutch the right hand of Mary. He is dressed in a green tunic, a red cincture, and a red cloak. He also wears sandals but the one on his right foot is loose so that it allows us to see the sole of his foot, perhaps a sign that, although God, he is also human. He has brown hair and childish features.

His feet and neck position appear to express a brusque movement caused by fear of something that he suddenly senses. What appears to have scared the Child is the vision of the Passion, represented by the cross and nails in the hands of the Archangel Gabriel.

The Archangel Michael presents Him with the other instruments of the Passion: the lance, the pole with a sponge and a vessel containing vinegar.

4. *The Mystery of Redemption*

The icon of Our Mother of Perpetual Help is not merely a decoration but a message. It is a dissertation about the central mystery of our faith. The different elements that appear in the icon, tell us about God-with-us, the way of the Cross, the loving intercession of Mary and the glory of Divine Light (the golden background).

In Mary's body the promise of salvation became a concrete reality when the Son of God took on our human nature. When the human life of her Son ended on the Cross, she was there as His first believer. It was in those last moments that Jesus designated her to be the Mother of all believers: "Behold, your mother" (John 19:27). Mary adopts us in order to bring us to Jesus.

The largest figure in the icon is that of Mary, but she is not the focal point of the painting. The center is rather in the joining of her hand with those of Jesus and the manner in which she points out that her Son is Jesus Christ, the Son of God who offers his life for us all.

This is a Marian icon with a message. It is a signpost on the road of life. Mary points out and directs us to Jesus.

The Child appears as a victim to be offered, much the same as in the Presentation in the Temple (Luke 2:22-40). The Mother's attitude reminds us of the Gospel words: "Mary stood at the foot of the Cross" (John 19:25), not collapsed in pain but erect, strong and valiant.

All the elements of the composition accentuate the reality of suffering, as is noted in the face of the Mother, the brusque movements of the Child and the instruments of the Passion. But, at the same time, there is an emphasis on the triumph of Jesus, depicted by the golden background and in the way that the angels carry the instruments of the Passion. More than threats of destruction, they appear as trophies of victory, as if they were taken from Calvary on Easter morning.

It is understandable why the image of Perpetual Help draws us to pray. It is a synthesis of the mysteries of Salvation. One can also understand why so many people like to pray the Rosary before the icon. They see in it not only the Virgin Mary, who accompanies us in our lives and prayers, but also the mysteries of the life of Christ: the Joyful Mysteries - (The Child), the Sorrowful Mysteries - (The Cross), and the Glorious Mysteries - (The Golden Background).

III. THE UNIVERSAL SCOPE
OF THE DEVOTION

On June 23, 1867, the image of Our Mother of Perpetual Help was crowned by the Dean of the Vatican Chapter. It was a solemn and official recognition of the Marian icon that had been rescued from oblivion.

Since then, devotion to the Mother of Perpetual Help has increasingly grown. One factor that contributed to this growth was the innumerable copies of the icon that were distributed from Rome throughout the world. On April 21, 1866, the Redemptorist Superior General gave one of the first copies of the icon to Pope Pius IX; this copy is now preserved in the chapel of the Redemptorists' General Government in Rome.

Another decisive factor in the spread of the devotion to Our Mother of Perpetual Help was that the Redemptorists made the icon a missionary and Marian image for the entire Congregation. This explains the presence of Perpetual Help in so many churches and homes throughout the world. Frequently it is distributed as a remembrance of a parish mission preached by Redemptorist Missionaries.

On May 23, 1871, the *Pious Union of Our Lady of Perpetual Help* was established in the Church of St. Alphonsus in Rome. In 1876, the *Archconfraternity of Our Lady of Perpetual Help and of St. Alphonsus Liguori* was formed, and the feast of Our Blessed Virgin Mary under the title of "Mother of Perpetual Help" was created. A special Mass and Breviary readings were composed for the celebration of the new feast day, the Sunday before the feast of St. John the Baptist. Afterwards, the 27th of June was fixed as the official feast day to honor Our Lady of Perpetual Help.

On December 25, 1878, in Santiago, Chile, the *Perpetual Intercession* was inaugurated and in 1928 the official beginning of the *Perpetual Novena* took place in the Church of St. Alphonsus, Saint Louis, Missouri (USA). (This Novena was actually started in 1922.)

1. *Why the Redemptorists?*

Why was this icon of the Mother of God given to the Redemptorists? There is no answer; some things are only understood by God and are seen as proofs of His love.

Humanly speaking, Pope Pius IX held the Redemptorists in high esteem. On one occasion at the tomb of St. Alphonsus, the Pope took off his papal ring to exchange it for the bishop's ring that the saint wore.

The Redemptorists were founded in 1732 to evangelize the poor and most abandoned. In the middle of the 19th century they were about to begin a period of growth that would carry them throughout the world. The Pope recognized that they would have the opportunity to make the icon known and proclaim, as had their founder, the glories of Mary. Thus he told them: *"Make her known throughout the world!"*

Beyond all human reasons, there was God's reason. Could it be that He wanted an intimate connection between a Congregation that has as its purpose the preaching of abundant Redemption and an icon that pictures this core message of Redemption?

The Church of St. Alphonsus, Rome.
Eucharistic celebration of the Feast of Perpetual Help, 1996.
From right to left: P. Juan M. Lasso de la Vega, Superior General of the Redemptorists; Bishop Mudryj Sofron, of the Greco-Byzantine rite, Ukraine; and Father Stanislaw Wróbel, General Consultor. One can appreciate the new setting for the Icon of Our Mother of Perpetual Help.

2. *The Church of Saint Alphonsus in Rome*

The church that houses the original icon of Perpetual Help is on the Via Merulana, very near the Basilica of St. Mary Major.

When the Italian Army of Unification conquered Rome in 1870, the Redemptorist house and church faced the threat of being expropriated. But once again, Our Mother of Perpetual Help providentially intervened on her own behalf, this time through a woman from the United States. This devotee of Mary found out that the wife of the American ambassador was coming to Rome. So she implored her to visit the Sanctuary of Perpetual Help. The illustrious visitor took a lively interest in helping the Redemptorists. Thus, in 1878, a favorable verdict guaranteed them definitive title to the house and church.

Among the many illustrious pilgrims of those first years were men and women like Mother Antonia de Oviedo (foundress of the Oblates of the Most Holy Redeemer), who donated the lamps that hang in the sanctuary, and Charles de Foucauld, who had come to Rome to renew his consecration to the Virgin of Perpetual Help.

The church's structure has undergone several modifications throughout the years. The facade was remodeled in 1898. In 1932, in order to accommodate the changes done to the Via Merulana, 24 steps were constructed in the atrium to improve the accessibility to the church. The latest restructuring of the main altar of the Virgin was done in 1995. In addition to daily liturgical celebrations, the Novena is celebrated every Wednesday afternoon for Polish pilgrims, and on Thursdays in English for the Filipino residents of Rome.

3. *The Basilica of Perpetual Help in Boston (USA)*

In February of 1870, the Redemptorist Missionaries of North America began construction on the first church dedicated to Our Lady of Perpetual Help. This wooden edifice was inaugurated on January 29, 1871.

As time passed, the church was unable to accommodate the growing number of Our Lady's devotees. A new church was planned. This second building, the present Basilica, was consecrated in April of 1878. The church is composed of three naves in perfect proportion: 65.6 meters long, 25 meters wide and 35 meters high. Two impressive spires, built in 1910, hold 12 huge bells. The main altar that holds the picture of Perpetual Help, was completed in 1896.

While conserving its traditional splendor, the Basilica has widened its pastoral ministry and is increasingly visited by Hispanics and Afro-Americans.

4. *The Basilica of Perpetual Help in Chile*

One of the first places in South America where the icon of Perpetual Help arrived was in Surinam. Blessed Peter Donders enthroned her image in the wooden chapel of the local leper colony.

Devotion to Perpetual Help began in Ecuador with the arrival of the Redemptorist missionaries. From there it spread along the Pacific coast of South America to Chile, Bolivia, Peru and Colombia.

At the southern end of the continent, in Santiago, Chile, an association of devotees of the Virgin of Perpetual Help,

The Basilica of Our Lady of Perpetual Help
Santiago, Chile

"Perpetual Intercession", was founded in 1879. Fifteen years later it numbered over 1,650 members. The Association had outgrown the size of its chapel, so plans for a larger church were developed. Thus rose the beautiful

Gothic church under the supervision of three Redemptorist Brothers: Gerard, Joachim and Hubert. It took 15 years to complete (1904-1919), and measures 68 meters long and 30 meters wide, with twin spires 48 meters high and a third, more slender spire 64 meters high. In 1926 it was declared a "Minor Basilica", the first church dedicated to Perpetual Help to receive this distinction.

The sonorous bells and the French organ of the Basilica have been praised for their "artistic value" by the local government.

5. *The Church of Baclaran in The Philippines*

Interior of the church, Baclaran - Manila

Since the arrival of the Redemptorist Missionaries in 1906, devotion to Our Lady of Perpetual Help spread throughout the Philippine Islands. In 1931, the foundation of the Redemptorist house and church in Baclaran, Manila was blessed with the Novena in her honor.

During World War II, Japanese troops expropriated the Redemptorist house and dispersed the religious community. The Fathers were able to save the icon of Perpetual Help and concealed it with friends. At the end of the war (1945), the Redemptorists returned to Baclaran. Much to their dismay, they found the house of these friends looted and burned. The image of the Virgin was nowhere to be found. After much prayer and searching, they finally discovered the icon in an Army warehouse. So the rescue operation was completed and the icon of Perpetual Help returned to her shrine and her public. The Perpetual Novena was first celebrated in Baclaran on June 23, 1948. In 1953, construction was begun on a new church as the people simply did not fit in the chapel. With the donations from Mary's devotees, the church was built and finally consecrated in December of 1958. From that date to the present, the church that holds some 11,000 persons has never closed its doors. It is open day and night to accommodate the many faithful that come around the clock to pray before the icon of the Virgin.

Fifty years ago, the Perpetual Novena began at Baclaran with 70 persons. Now, every Wednesday, some 100,000 faithful devotees of Mary come seeking her intercession. (On the first Wednesday of each month the crowds reach 120,000 devotees.) And this, considering that on Wednesdays in almost every church in the Philippines, the Perpetual Novena is celebrated!

6. *The Sanctuary of Curitiba, Brazil*

The Redemptorist presence in Curitiba is rather recent (1960). In the beginning, devotions to Our Lady of Perpetual Help were held in a small chapel. But after establishing the Perpetual Novena, so many people began to gather before the icon that they overflowed into the streets, interrupting the flow of traffic. The local government together with the Redemptorist community had to search for a solution to this "weekly" problem.

In 1966, the construction of the present sanctuary was begun in a nearby empty lot. The church, designed by a rather famous local architect, is circular in form with five doors. It was blessed and opened in June of 1969. Every Wednesday from 6:30 a.m. until 9:00 p.m. a total of 11 novena services are held, 5 of which are transmitted by radio throughout the city and rural areas nearby. There are also several Redemptorist Missionaries available the entire day for the Sacrament of Reconciliation and spiritual direction. The attendance each Wednesday is estimated at approximately 18,000 persons. The Perpetual Novena to Our Lady of Perpetual Help is thriving in many other areas of Brazil, from the city of Porto Alegre to the city of Araraquara, to Manaus on the Amazon River. Perhaps the church that has the highest participation at the Novena is the Redemptorist Church in Belém, Pará, in northeast Brazil, near the delta of the Amazon River, where the number of participants exceeds 20,000 persons each Wednesday.

"The face of our Lady of Fatima
was just like that of our Lady of Perpetual Help".
The words of Sister Lucia to Father Thomas Mc Glynn, O.P.

7. *The Redemptorist Church in Belfast, North Ireland*

From the earliest of Christian times, Ireland has been known as the cradle of missionaries. The Augustinians, who guarded the icon of Perpetual Help in St. Matthew's Church in Rome, were Irish. In more recent times, the Redemptorists have crisscrossed the length and breath of Ireland giving parish missions, recognized for their Marian devotion.

The Sanctuary of Perpetual Help in Limerick has been converted into a center of renewed devotion to the Mother of God. The annual novena sees more than 50,000 faithful participants daily. From Limerick the solemn celebration of the Novena has spread to the four corners of the land.

In Belfast, a city well known for tensions and violence between Catholics and Protestants, the Church of the Most Holy Redeemer is located directly on the dividing line between two conflicting neighborhoods. From its construction in 1911, this church has been the site of devotion to Our Lady of Perpetual Help, especially since 1943, when the Perpetual Novena began. Each year a Solemn Novena to Perpetual Help is held and daily attracts several thousands of devotees. What is particularly notable about this Novena is that for the last few years, a number of Protestant pastors, accompanied by some of their parishioners, have begun to participate. Presbyterians, Methodists and members of the Church of Ireland bring their beliefs before Mary, the Mother of Jesus, with warmth and eloquence.

This focus has converted the icon of the Virgin into a point for dialogue between Catholics and Protestants which is a source of ecumenism and social peace.

8. *The Shrine of Perpetual Help in Krakow, Poland*

The icon of Perpetual Help is well known and venerated throughout Eastern Europe: Poland, the Czech Republic, Slovakia, as well as the countries that formed part of the Soviet Union. Perhaps the most famous sanctuary of Our Lady of Perpetual Help in Poland is located in Krakow. The devotion began there in 1903, when the Redemptorists enthroned a copy of the icon blessed by Pope Leo XIII. The image began to draw people and inspire in them a deep devotion to Mary. The numbers of devotees became so great, that after two months the Archconfraternity of Our Lady of Perpetual Help and St. Alphonsus was founded.

There always are devotees before the altar of Our Lady. The young Karol Wojtyla (the future Pope John Paul II) frequently visited her after a day's work at the "Solvay" factory. During a visit made to the Sanctuary of Perpetual Help in Rome, in 1991, he recalled those times: "I remember that during World War II, during the time of the Nazi occupation of Poland, I was a factory worker in Krakow. On my way home, after work, since it was on my way, I always stopped at the Redemptorist church. In the church there was the picture of Perpetual Help. I used to stop there, not only because it was on my way, but because that picture just seemed so beautiful. And I kept visiting that church even after I was named bishop and cardinal".

On June 26, 1994, during a well attended ceremony, Cardinal Macharski solemnly placed the Papal Crown on the icon of Perpetual Help of Krakow.

9. *The Novena Church in Singapore*

*The Feast of Our Lady of Perpetual Help in Singapore.
A floral arrangement with the words: "Make her known".*

If you ever have the opportunity to visit the city of Singapore, be sure to take the subway to the "Novena" station. There you will find the Church of St. Alphonsus, although everyone knows it as "The Novena Church". Every Saturday more than 20,000 people gather for the celebrations of the Perpetual Novena.

Interestingly, Singapore is a Buddhist country and many of the participants in the Novenas are not Catholic. Yet Our Lady of Perpetual Help seems to take charge of preparing for them a way to her Son. The main Center for Pre-evangelization and the Catecumenate is located at the Shrine.

10. *Haiti: a Nation Consecrated to Perpetual Help*

In 1881 the Caribbean country of Haiti was afflicted with a terrible epidemic of smallpox. The scourge was particularly horrible in the capital city of Port-au-Prince. At the beginning of 1882 the plague intensified. The doctors saw no other solution to ease the situation than intense rain storms to cleanse the atmosphere. But that time of year in Haiti was known as the "dry season".

A copy of the postage stamp issued in Haiti
to commemorate the centenary of the miracle.

One woman had brought a copy of the image of Perpetual Help from France and offered it to the Rector of the Cathedral of Port-au-Prince, hoping that invoking the Holy Virgin would alleviate the horrible plague. On February 5, a solemn procession was held during which the image of Perpetual Help was carried to a small chapel overlooking the city. The Novena began. On February 10, contrary to all weather predictions, several cloudbursts occurred. From that moment the epidemic began to diminish: no new contagious cases were reported and the afflicted began to recover.

In the collective consciousness of the people, there was no doubt that Our Lady of Perpetual Help had answered their prayers and saved the city. Since then she is called "The Virgin of the Miracle".

The picture of their "Protectress" is found in almost every home of the country. The National Bishops' Conference and the civil government have officially placed the Haitian nation under the patronage of Perpetual Help.

11. *Perpetual Help in Mexico*

In many parts of Latin America copies of the icon of Our Lady of Perpetual Help arrived before the Redemptorist Missionaries, e.g. Argentina, Paraguay, Venezuela, Central America and the Caribbean. But the widespread devotion to Her is due to Redemptorist missions preached in so many parishes and it is not difficult to believe that in some areas there is hardly a home that does not have a picture of Perpetual Help. Due to the popularity of Perpetual Help in

Latin America, she is sometimes called: "The Missionary Virgin" or "The Star of the New Evangelization".

In Mexico the first copy of the icon appeared in the Cathedral of Morelia, Michoacán. In Mexico City the first altar dedicated to Our Lady of Perpetual Help was in the Church of San Diego, and was subsequently moved to the neighboring church of The Holy Cross.

After the arrival of the Redemptorists in Mexico (1908), the devotion spread throughout the towns and villages in an extraordinary manner. Her presence is also seen in the capital city in the Redemptorist parish of the Holy Redeemer.

There are several churches in Mexico dedicated to Our Lady of Perpetual Help. Special mention should be made of the shrines in Monterrey, Torreón, San Luis Potosí, as well as the modern church of Perpetual Help in Ciudad Hidalgo and the recently built church in Acapulco. In Lomas de los Viñedos, Tequisquiapan, Querétaro, there stands a beautiful sanctuary dedicated to Our Lady of Perpetual Help.

The profound faith that the Mexican nation has for the Virgin of Guadalupe is well known. With the passing of the years, this devotion has been converted into a symbol of national identity. But devotion to Our Lady of Perpetual Help is not seen as competition to the Virgin of Guadalupe; rather, the faithful understand that the "Dark Virgin", the Mother of Jesus and Mother of the Faithful, is always ready to help her sons and daughters.

The Church of Our Lady of Perpetual Help
Tequisquiapan, Querétaro, Mexico

12. *A Universal Devotion*

During several centuries the icon of Perpetual Help was only known in Rome. But since 1866 her presence and the devotion have been spread marvelously throughout the world due, not only to the favors Mary has conceded to so many of her faithful children, but also to the preaching of the Redemptorist Missionaries. To get an idea of her popularity one need only to notice her presence in the rural and urban areas of France, Austria, Germany, Belgium, Holland, Spain, Portugal, to mention just a few European countries.

There are innumerable parishes with the title of Perpetual

Help. A glance at the Diocesan Directories is sufficient to see that Her name appears all over the world - Vancouver, Kansas City, New York, Brooklyn, Madrid, Cape Town, Mumbai (Bombay), the sanctuary in Bussolengo (near Verona, Italy) and the parishes of Perpetual Help in the poor areas of Montevideo, Uruguay and Lima, Peru.

In the Pontifical Directory, there is a listing of six religious congregations of Sisters with the name of "Our Lady of Good Help", and three with the title of "Our Lady of Perpetual Help". And that is without counting the religious congregations and institutes on the national or diocesan levels. In the Melkite Orthodox Rite (not in union with Rome), there is a community of Sisters with the title of "Missionary Religious of Our Lady of Perpetual Help", founded in 1936. There are

also many educational centers, hospitals, centers for human development, etc. that carry the name of Our Lady of Perpetual Help. In Portugal, for example, there is a large center for social services: health care, formal education and spiritual formation, named: "Our Lady of Perpetual Help Care Center". In Biblos, Lebanon, the Catholic Maronite hospital is dedicated to Perpetual Help.

There are also many Catholic magazines that bear the name of Perpetual Help in the United States, Spain, Mexico, Italy, etc.

41

IV. FAVORS AND DEVOTIONS

A. FAVORS AND GRACES

The "Miraculous" Icon

The holy image of the Mother of Perpetual Help was returned to public veneration on April 26, 1866. On that day a solemn procession was held, carrying the icon from the Basilica of St. Mary Major to the Church of St. Alphonsus. The following is taken from the chronicles of the Shrine:

"On one of the streets along the route of the procession, there lived a 4 year old boy, who had been seriously ill for some 20 days. He suffered from a gastric infection and brain hemorrhages. It seemed that he was very near death. When the icon passed in front of his house, his mother opened the window and presented him to the Virgin, exclaiming with tears: "O merciful Mother, heal my son or take him with you to Paradise!" Her prayer was not in vain; on the same day the child improved noticeably and a few days later was completely cured.

"In another house there was an eight year old girl that for the last four years had suffered from paralysis of the legs and could hardly move them. When the icon passed her house, her mother asked the Virgin to cure her daughter. At that same moment, the girl recovered partial use of her legs. Afterwards, the mother took the girl to the Church of St. Alphonsus and presented her to the Virgin. Full of confidence, she exclaimed: "O Mother, finish now what you have begun!" To the great surprise and wonder of those present, the girl stood up and began to walk on her own".

It is understandable that the faithful began to speak of "the miraculous picture" of Our Lady of Perpetual Help. What that term means would depend on the intentions and circumstances of each person that uses it. But the fact is that in order to describe Mary's favorable answer to their prayers, there is a constant expression used: "miraculous intercession". And it is used so frequently that one could think that the Virgin of the icon is always disposed to grant extraordinary favors.

The Gospel of St. John tells us that the first miracle of Jesus, performed during the wedding feast at Cana, was done because of the petition of Mary, His mother. This is the meaning of the Perpetual Help "miracles": they happen through the intercession of Mary before her Son. Mary is always the Mother that holds her Son Jesus, but at the same time, looks solicitously at her other sons and daughters. Favor and grace are the expressions of the Divine Motherhood of Mary. The circumstances of human life offer her the opportunity for granting them. They are signs of her help in times of every-day troubles, her way to accompany her sons and daughters in every moment of need.

In these pages we are not using the word "miracle" in the theological sense as when we speak of the miracles of Jesus or the miracles recognized by the Church in the process of canonization of the Saints. Here we use the word "miracle" in a wider sense as used by the faithful. It is not a question of dogmas of faith but rather, experiences of faith. In this Christian sense, these "miracles" also have norms of certitude. In the idiom of the faithful a miracle is a grace, a help, a protection, a favor asked for and received, an experience of inner peace.

2. *Testimonials of thanksgiving*

Some miracles awaken feelings of wonder by emphasizing the spectacular. But the favors received through the intercession of Our Lady of Perpetual Help seem to awaken profound feelings of gratitude to the Heavenly Father, who has listened to the prayers of the Mother of His Son as she intercedes on behalf of all her needy sons and daughters.

One of the most impressive moments in the Perpetual Novena is precisely the reading of a few of the letters received: some give thanks to God and the Virgin for favors received, others plead for their intentions. With all simplicity, ordinary people recount their problems confidently asking for the Virgin's help or expressing their gratitude for favors received. If we published the details of the healing, the help in time of troubles and the moments of protection, the list would be endless. To the list of favors publicly acknowledged, we would have to also add those favors that have been received but guarded in the silence of the hearts of so many of Mary's devotees.

The following three letters are samples of those received from around the world.

From a mother: My son was born premature, in his sixth month, and put into an incubator with very little hope of surviving... I asked Our Lady of Perpetual Help to protect him, to let him not suffer and that whatever was best for him would happen. I knew that she would help me, since I always make the Novena. After eleven days, they called me from the hospital to tell me that my son was dying. My husband and I went desperately to the hospital and found the child dead. That was when I begged Our Lady to receive my son in her arms, since this was the Will of God. When I embraced my dead son, my heart was breaking with such pain that only a mother could feel. After a few minutes of this horrible suffering, and realizing there was nothing else to be done, we could hardly believe our eyes: the baby began to breathe again! He was kept for two more months in the incubator before we could take him home. Today he is in good health. I will never stop thanking God and Our Lady for this grace which I consider a miracle.

From a young woman in the Philippines: Dearest Mother of Perpetual Help: I remember perfectly the day that I came to the Novena for the first time. It was two years ago in June. At that time I needed help in a special way and knew that no one else but you could give it to me... I had gotten a job, but family matters were not going well and I couldn't concentrate on what I should have been doing. That is why I promised you that I would come to the Novena, not just for nine Wednesdays, but every Wednesday of my life. And my prayers were answered. My father found work and my sisters could go back to their studies.

Last January, my life and our family matters took a turn for the worst. That is why I stopped coming to the Novena. It seemed that I could always find an easy excuse not to come. The truth of the matter is that I met a man and fell madly in love with him. I was so afraid of losing him that I wasn't willing to face anything that would separate us, but without realizing that my whole life was getting totally mixed up. I became irritable and very insecure...

After a tremendous struggle, I decided to come back to the Novena and stopped seeing my friend for a while. In October, I learned that he had another fiancée and had married her. I fell into a horrible depression. I broke off relations with my family and seriously considered leaving my job. But despite all this, I continued coming to the Novena. It is only now that I realize that you did answer my petitions: my family is well, my sisters are back in school and I... was freed of a person that would have caused me untold sorrow. I only ask now that you help me heal the wounds that I caused myself.

Thank you dear Mother. Right now I feel that things are getting better and that my life has more meaning.

From a grateful family: Exactly two months ago our four year old daughter was rushed to the hospital and had to stay there for forty-three days due to a brain disease called leuco-encephalitis. She is now fully recovered. She has gained weight, is lovable and happy; she sings, talks, shouts, laughs, plays, walks and considering all that she has suffered, it seems that there is no sign of any damage from her sickness. We consider this a miracle, since the doctors warned us that if she would survive, she would probably be blind, deaf or mentally retarded.

We want to thank your beloved Son, Jesus Christ, for having allowed us to unite our sufferings to His. And we thank you, dear Mother of Perpetual Help, for all the benefits given to our daughter, and through her, to us. We beg you to guide and protect us always. We love you.

Many other testimonies such as these could be recorded, signs of the constant intercession of Mary, which make visible the unique and eternal mediation of her Son. The Second Vatican Council says: "In her motherly love she looks after the sisters and brothers of her Son who are still on their pilgrimage and placed amidst danger and difficulties, until they are led to their happy homeland. Therefore in the Church the blessed Virgin is invoked by the titles of advocate, benefactress, helper and mediatrix" (*Dogmatic Constitution on the Church,* n° 62).

B. Prayers to Our Mother of Perpetual Help

1. INVOCATIONS

Leader: O Mother of Perpetual Help, You whose very name inspires confidence!
R: *Help me, O loving Mother.*

That I may be victorious in the times of trial and temptation. R: *Help me, O loving Mother.*
That I may quickly rise again should I have the misfortune to fall into sin. R: *Help me...*
That I may break asunder any bonds of Satan in which I may become entangled. R: *Help me...*
That in hearing the Word of God, I may live according to it. R: *Help me...*
That I may live all my days as a faithful follower of Jesus Christ. R: *Help me...*
That I may make of my entire life a loving service to God and neighbor. R: *Help me...*
In all the trials and troubles of life. R: *Help me...*
Against my own inconstancy, that I may persevere to the end. R: *Help me...*
O Mother, to my last hour, to my last breath, watch over me. R: *Help me...*

All: May you be loved, / may you be praised, / may you be invoked, / may you be eternally blessed, / O Mother of Perpetual Help, / my hope, my love, my mother, / my refuge and my life. / Amen.

2. PRAYER

O Holy Virgin Mary * who to inspire us with boundless confidence * has been pleased to take the sweet name of Our Mother of Perpetual Help * I implore You * to come to my aid always and everywhere * in my temptations * after my falls * in my difficulties * in all the miseries of life * and above all, at the hour of my death. * Give me, O loving Mother the desire * and the habit * always to have recourse to You trusting that * You will be faithful and come to my assistance. * Obtain for me then this grace of graces * the grace to pray to You * without ceasing and with childlike confidence * that I may ensure Your perpetual help * and final perseverance. * O Mother of Perpetual Help * pray for me now and at the hour of my death. * Amen.

(Our Father, Hail Mary, Glory be...)

One of the interesting elements of the icon of Perpetual Help is the sandal falling from the foot of the Christ Child. There are different explanations about this detail.

Artistic: in many icons, to show the sole of the foot is equivalent to showing the human nature of the person represented.

Medical: the degree of a person's consciousness can be perceived according to the reflexes as manifested in the sole of the foot (Babinski's Reflex). A sudden movement in the nape of the neck causes a reflex in one of the inferior extremities (Brudzinski's Reflex).

Cultural: In ancient Israel, when someone wanted to cede their rights to another, he would take off his sandal and give it to the beneficiary (Cf. Ruth 4:7-8).

C. A Short Novena to Our Mother of Perpetual Help

1. *Prayer for Each Day*
(Looking at her Image)

O Mary, Mother of Jesus and our Mother of Perpetual Help, during these nine days I am going to look to you to discover in your Icon, the outstanding symbols, the important lessons, the mysterious nuances that Your inspired artist wanted to depict in Your picture. I am not only going to learn about them in these pages, but also try to learn, O admirable Teacher, what You want to teach me about Your Son and about our God, father and mother of all love.

Help me to faithfully follow Your Son, Jesus Christ. Awaken in my understanding and in my heart, the faith, hope and love with which You want me to behold you and invoke you so that I live with unlimited confidence in Your perpetual help. Amen. *(Hail Mary...)*

2. *Meditation for Each Day*

(Read the text that corresponds to each day)

3. *Final prayer* *(composed by Pope John Paul II)*

O Virgin of Perpetual Help, great sign of our hope, Holy Mother of the Redeemer, we invoke your name. Help your people who desire to be renewed. Give us joy as we walk towards the future in conscious and active solidarity with the poorest of our brothers and sisters, announcing to them in a new and courageous way, the Gospel of Your Son, the beginning and the end of all human relationships that aspire to live a true, just and lasting peace. As does the Child Jesus, Whom we admire in this venerable icon, so we also want to hold your right hand. You have both the power and the goodness to help us in every need and circumstance of life. This moment is yours. Come then, and help us; be for us our refuge and our hope. Amen.

THE FIRST DAY
Contemplating the Archangel Gabriel

Mother of Perpetual Help, the Archangel Gabriel of the Annunciation, appears in your icon carrying a cross and nails. He reminds us of Nazareth; it was he who descended to one of the fifty humble homes of the village. There he met you and announced the Incarnation: that the Son of God, by act of the Holy Spirit, would make Himself our Brother by becoming in your womb one with us in our human nature.

In Nazareth you raised Jesus in an atmosphere of simplicity and work. You, Mother, used to take Jesus' hands in yours to teach Him to pray; you taught Him the Psalms and the prayers of your people.

Dearest Mother, servant of the Lord and simple housewife, teach us to love our homes and fill them with joy and understanding. Help us to build a society that is both just and fraternal, where there is bread and work for all.

THE SECOND DAY
Contemplating the Archangel Michael

On your right, at the level of your shoulders, we see the Archangel Michael, leader of the celestial armies and zealous defender of the Lord's glory. He reminds us that only God is Lord of the Universe and that His Kingdom is a kingdom of justice, love and peace.

The Archangel holds a sponge and a lance in the folds of his green mantel. With the sponge, the lips of your dying Son were moistened as His mouth and throat burned with thirst. With the lance, His side was pierced and from it flowed water and blood. But your Son did not die a failure; on the third day His Heavenly Father raised Him up. From then on, the lance, the sponge and the cross have become the symbols of Jesus' victory over sin and death. What were signs of disgrace are now symbols of triumph.

O Mother of Perpetual Help, give us faith in the power of Your Son and in the purifying and restoring power of his sacred blood. He gave his life for everyone because his strength was anchored in love.

THE THIRD DAY
Contemplating the Letters on the Icon

On both sides of your haloed head, we see some large letters. They are the initials that mean "Mother of God". And next to the head of your Divine Son, there are some initials that mean "Jesus Christ".

Because you are the Mother of the Son of God made man, Jesus Christ, you are also our Perpetual Help, our certain, tireless intercessor; you are the powerful means to obtain what we ask you. You are the Mother of God. That is your unique, incomparable title.

There are many mothers with illustrious sons, even as there are innumerable women of great influence in the areas of power, the arts and the sciences. But you are the one that we praise, we venerate and rejoice in, above all other creatures. As God continues to show us His mercy through you generation after generation, we call you "Blessed".

Holy Mary, "blessed among all women", pray for us.

THE FOURTH DAY
Contemplating the Left Hand of Mary

The instruments of the Passion (lance, sponge, nails and cross) are in the hands of the Angels. In your left hand you hold the Child Jesus. In this icon, Nazareth and Calvary, the infancy and the redemptive death of Jesus, are united.

As you presented your Son in the Temple, Simeon told you that a sword would pierce your soul. And from that moment, Mary, nor a day passed without your thinking of the meaning of those words. You cherished the baby talk of Jesus, His first faltering steps and, later on, His independence. But you always saw in Him the shadow of a sword hanging over His head, a sword that deeply saddened you.

Mother of Perpetual Help, you are holding Jesus against your heart. Sustain us in our weakness as we look to the future and perhaps see it darkened by sickness and pain. We trust in your protection, because your very title of Perpetual Help is an invitation to confidence and hope.

THE FIFTH DAY
Contemplating 'Hand in Hand'

With your left hand, you hold the Child Jesus. With your right, you take the hands of the Child, while your long, slender fingers point to His face. One day in Cana you said: "Do what He tells you". You point to Jesus, all good and all powerful. Through your image you remind us that you are only the one that points out the road, the guide, the Virgin of the Way.

Our Heavenly Father said at the moment of the Transfiguration: "This is my beloved Son, listen to Him". Mary, you are the sign that allows us to identify the loving and comforting presence of Jesus. Where He is, you are, inseparable. You tell us, Mary, Mother and first disciple of

Jesus, that to be a Christian consists of following your Son and that you will take us by the hand to Him.

Thank you Mother, for lighting our way to our Father's House. Strengthen our faith and enliven our hope when we tire on life's journey.

THE SIXTH DAY
Contemplating the Child in Your Arms

Well do we see Him. He is no longer a baby but has already lived a few years.

We go back to think about Nazareth and its ordinary and peaceful home life. You dedicated yourself to your domestic chores: the kitchen and the oven, providing water and fire-wood, taking Jesus by the hand to the village well. What a nice place to meet friends, talk awhile, comment on the village news. Meanwhile the children played and, among them, Jesus. With Joseph and Jesus you formed a simple family in a humble town of Israel.

Good Mother, enlighten us to recognize the presence of Our Heavenly Father even in the fatigue of our daily life. He never lets go of our hand, even when our faith seems to falter or we are overcome by difficulties. Strengthen us so that, full of confidence, we can ask Him, as Jesus taught us, for our daily bread, and not to let us fall into temptation and despair.

THE SEVENTH DAY
Contemplating the Star

On your head, gracious Mother, we see a star. It reminds us of the star that guided the Wise Men of the Orient to Bethlehem to worship the Infant Jesus. You are like that Star of Bethlehem: you guide us to Jesus and point out where we can find Him - in His Word, in the Eucharist, in the silence of prayer, and in our brothers and sisters, and especially, in the poor and abandoned.

After the Resurrection of your Son, you accompanied the first disciples in vigilant prayer. Thus you were among the Apostles at Pentecost, when the Holy Spirit began the preaching of the Good News to the whole world. You accompanied the new Church in its first missionary steps.

Holy Mary, Star of Evangelization, help us to fulfill our mission as followers of your Son. Bless the efforts of all who proclaim the Good News.

THE EIGHTH DAY
Contemplating the Colors of the Icon

Your icon, Holy Mother, is made up of contrasts. The Child's sandal is falling while His hands are tightly clutching yours. The instruments of the Passion are carried, wrapped in a cloak, as if they were just collected after the Resurrection. The colors that the artist chose accentuate these contrasts: the blue, red and green of the clothing and the gold background.

The tunic you are wearing is red and the cloak that

covers it is blue. Did the artist want to remind us that you are a created person (red), but at the same time recalling that the Holy Spirit covered you with His Presence and grace (blue)? On the other hand, the Child wears a green tunic, while His cloak and sash are in shades of red. Is this a sign that He is the Divine Life (green) that has taken on our humanity (red)?

The artist distinguishes five levels of depth in the icon. The first level: the hand that points to the Savior. Then the Child - Jesus Christ. The third level is your own presence. Further back are the angels with the instruments of the Passion. And as a general background, the golden light. Since this icon is about Our Savior, it shows him in Nazareth, on Calvary and in his glory.

Mary, teach me to live the contrasts of life with optimism, the birthing and dying that goes on each day. Help me to understand more of the mystery of our salvation that passes through cross and pain to reach triumph and Resurrection.

THE NINTH DAY
Contemplating the Eyes of Mary

We end this wonderful novena of discovering in your image the reason for your name. It is all present in your eyes. You are our Perpetual Help because of your eyes, those eyes that follow us from left to right, that see us from any point from which we seek you. They watch us as eyes filled with love and a desire to protect us. They follow us perpetually, whatever our situation be, our detours, our absences, our returns.

You are our Perpetual Help because, as the icon shows us, your gesture of sustaining Jesus is eternal, since you now are forever at His side as our faithful intercessor. To be Perpetual Help is your mission, Mediatrix of God's inexhaustible grace, despite the immensity of our faults.

Grant us the favor of responding to your Perpetual Help by always coming to you in persevering prayer.

Stained glass window in the Redemptorist Church
San Salvador, Central America

1. OPENING HYMN

Immaculate Mother
We join you and call
On God our dear Father
The Lord of us all.
Ave, Ave, Ave Maria
Ave, Ave, Ave Maria.

>In God's Holy Spirit
>Your children are we
>Inspire us, our model
>Good Christians to be.
>Ave, Ave, Ave Maria
>Ave, Ave, Ave Maria.

Leader: In the name of the Father and of the Son and of the Holy Spirit. *All*: Amen.

Leader: My brothers and sisters, we are gathered together before the picture of our Mother of Perpetual Help, to praise and thank God our Father for the blessings He has given us through her intercession. Let us once more ask her to pray for us.

2. NOVENA PRAYER

All: Mother of Perpetual Help *look on us your children. We are proud to be your children *and happy to call you our mother. We are not all we ought to be so we come to you our mother. You are always ready to accept us as we are, *to encourage us to do better, *in spite of temptation and weakness.

As we look at your picture, *we remember your life on earth. You had many crosses and trials *but you knew how to face them. You had faith and trust in God. You relied on his loving, fatherly goodness. Help us to be like you. We too have our trials and troubles. We are often worried and confused. Give us courage. Strengthen our faith.

Help us make one more effort when we are inclined to despair. As you stood at the foot of the cross *you found it hard to see how God could allow his Son *to suffer such agony. Yet you never lost faith. Help us to learn from your example to face our trials *with confidence and trust in God.

Sometimes loving mother, *we are so worried about our own problems *we forget about God and needs of others. We want to be like you. You forgot about yourself and your own problems *when you saw others in need. Help us to remember *that the troubles and sorrows of the others *are sometimes greater than our own. So, Mother Mary, *while we pray with you for our own special intention *we include those of all your children in need: *the sick and the dying, *the lonely and the broken hearted, *the poor and the oppressed, *in a word, all who need your perpetual help. Amen.

3. LITANY OF PETITIONS

Leader: Our Mother of Perpetual Help, your children call on you.
Response: Mother ever help us.

That you may ever be our inspiration...
That we may have courage to face up to all our difficulties...
That we may see meaning in the joys and sorrows of life...
That our trust in God may help others too...

When faced with difficult decisions...
When asked to a make a sacrifice for the sake of others...
When put to shame in front of others...
When hurt and tempted to take revenge...

In times of sickness in the home...
In worries about our financial difficulties...
In misunderstandings with those we love...
In helping young people to become self-reliant...

That many may respond to God's call to the priesthood or religious life especially to the Redemptorist Congregation...

In choosing our entertainment and recreation...

That parents may learn to adapt to their growing children...

That students may show appreciation to those who sacrifice for their education...

That teachers may always be inspired in forming their students to become better Christians...

That we may not resort to drugs or drink as an escape from life...

That we may always be honest in the struggle to earn our livelihood...

That we may not be driven by greed for power and wealth...

That we may always take pride in doing our work well...

That workers may be justly rewarded for their labor...

That we and lending agencies, in the guise of helping others may not destroy people by collecting unjust high interest rates...

That we may never interfere with justice by bribery or perjury...

That we may rise above personal considerations when called on to serve the community (or to love)...

That we may never lose sight of the beauty of our country and the goodness of our people...

That we may do everything in our power to bring about justice, peace and progress in our land...

That we may never be so proud as to think we can do without God or religion...

When seriously ill and we realize that death is near...

When our loved ones are called home to their heavenly Father...

When we pray that our dear departed may share in the full joy of Christ's resurrection...

And now in silence let us pray for our special intentions... *(pause)*

Leader: Let us pray.

All: Holy Mary, you always help those in need, you cheer those who weep, you encourage those who have lost hope and help them lead good Christian lives. Join with us now as we ask our Father for guidance.

4. THANKSGIVING PRAYER *(All Stand)*

Leader: Let us now thank our Mother of Perpetual Help for the favors that we and others have received through her intercession.

All: O Mother of Perpetual Help *with grateful hearts we join you *in thanking God *for all the wonderful things *He has done for us, especially for having given us Jesus your Son *as our Redeemer.

O God our Creator *we thank you for the gift of life and all the gifts of nature: *our senses and faculties, *our talents and abilities. We thank you for creating us in your image and likeness *and for giving us this earth to use and develop, *to respect and cherish. Despite our failures *you continue to show your love for us today *by increasing the life of your spirit in us.

Finally, we thank you loving Father *for giving us Mary the Mother of your Son *to be our Mother of Perpetual Help. We are grateful for all the favors *we have received through her intercession. We pray that those past favors may inspire us *to greater confidence in your loving mercy *and to seek the aid of our Mother of Perpetual Help. Amen.

Hymn to Mary *(Suggested Hymn: Hail Mary or The Magnificat)*

5. MASS IN HONOR
OF OUR MOTHER OF PERPETUAL HELP

Priest: In the name of the Father, and of the Son and of the Holy Spirit. Amen.

Priest: May the grace and peace of our Lord Jesus Christ, the love of God and the fellowship of the Holy Spirit be with you all.
All: And also with you.

Priest: My brothers and sisters, we celebrate this Eucharist in honor of our Mother of Perpetual Help. Since we are not sinless, let us first ask pardon for our sins.

Priest: Because we have not responded to your love for us, Lord have mercy. *All*: Lord have mercy.

Priest: Because we have been ungrateful to you, Christ have mercy. *All*: Christ have mercy.

Priest: Because we have been selfish and forgetful of the needs of others, Lord have mercy. *All*: Lord have mercy.

Priest: May Almighty God have mercy on us, forgive us our sins and bring us to everlasting life. *All*: Amen.

Opening Prayer

Priest: Let us pray. Lord God, give your people the joy of continual health of mind and body. With the prayers of Mary, our Mother of Perpetual Help, guide us through the sorrows of this life to eternal happiness in the life to come. Grant this through Jesus Christ, Your son who lives and reigns with you and the Holy spirit, one God, forever and ever. Amen.

Liturgy Of The Eucharist

Preparation of the Gifts
(Hymn: "Here we gather" or other suitable hymn)

Lord God, we honor the memory of the mother of your Son. May the sacrifice we share make us an everlasting gift to you. We ask this through Christ our Lord. Amen.

Eucharistic Prayer

(The preface is that most apt to the season of the church's year or the preface to Our Lady)

Prayer after Communion

Lord we rejoice in your sacraments and ask your mercy as we honor the memory of the Virgin Mary, our Mother of Perpetual Help. May her faith and love inspire us to serve you more faithfully in the work of salvation. Grant this in the name of Jesus the Lord. Amen.

6. FINAL BLESSING

Priest: The Lord be with you.
All: And also with you.
Priest: Bow your heads for God's blessings.
May the Lord be with you to defend you. *All:* Amen.
Within you to preserve you. *All:* Amen.
Before you to lead you. *All:* Amen.
After you to bless you. *All:* Amen.
In the Name of the Father and of the Son and of the Holy Spirit. *All:* Amen.
Priest: The mass is ended. Let us go as God's people to serve one another.
All: Thanks be to God.

7. FINAL HYMN TO MARY
("Mother of Christ" or another suitable hymn)

Mother of Christ
Mother of Christ, Mother of Christ
What shall I ask of thee
I do not sigh for the wealth of earth
for the joys that fade and flee.
But, Mother of Christ, Mother of Christ
This do I long to see
The bliss untold which thine arms enfold
The treasure upon thy knee.

CONTENTS